D0820371

CATegories

Chosen and
introduced by # CAT
ROSALIE MANDER

Foreword by A.L.ROWSE

Illustrations by RICHARD KENNEDY

egories

Cats according to their characters from Sphinx, Gib-Hunter, Grimalkin, Tabby to Puss

Weidenfeld & Nicolson
London

Copyright © 1981 by Rosalie Mander

First published in Great Britain in 1981 by
George Weidenfeld and Nicolson Limited
91 Clapham High Street, London SW4 7TA

All rights reserved. No part of this publication
may be reproduced, stored in a retrieval system,
or transmitted, in any form or by any means,
electronic, mechanical, photocopying, recording
or otherwise, without the prior permission of
the copyright owner.

Book design by Joyce Chester

ISBN 0 297 77946 X

Printed in Great Britain by
Butler & Tanner Ltd
Frome and London

TO MISS T. C.

Without whom, sitting Sphinx-like on the desk or playing 'with sportive grace', kittenish on the keys, this book would have been finished much sooner.

CONTENTS

GIB-HUNTER

TABBY

Contents

FOREWORD
A.L.Rowse

CATS are perfect writers' animals. No wonder so many writers have been addicted to them, or have written well about them. There they are, silent companions, curled up or sleeping nearby, or sitting up beside one without interrupting or for ever pestering one, like a dog, to be taken out for a walk.

Not that I dislike dogs; I am fond of dogs – some dogs: not all. With them I discriminate, according to kind and conduct. I am devoted to all cats – and they know it.

Cats and dogs are *not* mutually exclusive, and it is not only possible but right to respond to both. Here, as elsewhere, it is not difficult to enjoy the pleasures, and reap the rewards, of ambivalence.

At the moment I am engaged in seducing a semi-wild tom-cat, Flip, who is semi-attached to the farm at Trenarren. He was really in love with the farmdog, Spot, no one else. Looking out of the window one day I saw an extraordinary spectacle: Flip sitting up on his behind simply pounding Spot's chest with paws and affection, the dog putting up with it with a fatuous expression of complacency on his face. When he tired of these pressing attentions, Flip simply pursued him: he *loved* Spot.

Someone went into the barn down below in the valley, to see Spot lying there surrounded by all the farm cats: a happy family. Now that dear old Spot is dead, I have a chance with Flip, who is coming round to me.

Dogs have been brain-washed by humans; one can almost always tell what they are thinking. And they take on the ridiculous aspects of humans. How often, when one sees some people with their dogs, one thinks, 'Really the dogs look as fatuous as their owners!' No one *owns* a cat; and they never look ridiculous.

Anthropologists tell us that cats became semi-attached to man earlier in the scheme of things than dogs, and hence have retained much more independence. More mysterious, more subtle, they are more of a challenge to humans – at any rate to intelligent ones.

It speaks for itself, when one notices what remarkable people have been attached to cats. I learn from Lady Mander that that very remarkable man, Mohammet, had the right attitude to them. A similar story, about cutting off a piece of his robe not to disturb a cat, is told of the great Cardinal Richelieu. All true cat-lovers share that impulse not to disturb a cat. I wonder why? – very mysterious.

It is a sign of goodness in the great that they have this sensibility – not only Mohammet and Richelieu, but Abraham Lincoln and Winston Churchill. No such sign with Hitler or Stalin or Mussolini, Krushchev or Brezhnev! They would all have been better men if only. . . . And, come to think of it, the one defect in that great woman, Elizabeth I, is that I know no evidence that she was fond of cats. (She was a bit of a cat herself, so was Richelieu – with a great cat's pounce.)

It is a singular gap in Shakespeare's universal charity that he does not seem to have liked cats or dogs. T.S.Eliot and Thomas Hardy, dear men, liked both – though Hardy wrote the more movingly, with grief for his cat. (His spoiled dog 'Wessex' bit a whole generation of writers.)

Rosalie Mander has confined herself to what has been written in, or translated into, English. Wonderful things are spoken of cats, in French, by such diverse writers as Baudelaire and Gautier and Colette. I can hardly believe that there is such a civilised response in German or Russian literature.

Here in this charming book we have the widest spectrum all the way from ancient Egypt or medieval England and Wales, to that good, forlorn, forgotten poet, Tessimond. Rosalie Mander is very learned in the lore of cats – as I am not: I just love them. I hope that that is enough, and will win me a place with them in Paradise.

Sphinx

INTRODUCTION
Thine is the lore of Ra and Rameses.

G.R.TOMSON

THE cat on the mat or lulled into sleep in the best armchair by the dying fall of his own last purr has been them all: each in its category. In a moment he can become any of them again: from Sphinx, the ancient deity called Bast; Gib-Hunter, terror of rodent and fowl; Grimalkin, familiar of the dusk; Tabby, or Moggy, the 'harmless necessary cat'; to Puss, the pet.

In each guise he must be approached with respect by ailourophile and ailourophobe alike in the code that T.S.Eliot laid down:

> I bow, and taking off my hat,
> Ad-dress him in this form, O Cat.

For behind those disdainful eyes there is ever the knowledge that he was once the Bast that St Clement of Alexandria reported seeing when he visited the great Temple. He was led up to a shrine concealed by curtains of hammered gold which attendant priests drew aside in fear and adoration. When he dared to raise his eyes he saw a purple cushion on which lay a cat drowsily licking its paws. It was the god-beast of whom it is written in the Book of the Dead:

> 'I am the Cat which fought hard by the Persea Tree
> In Annu, on the night when the foes of NEB-ER-Tcher
> were destroyed.
> Who then is this?
> The Male CAT is RA himself, and he is called MAU
> By reason of the speech of the god SA,
> Who said concerning him:
> He is like unto which he hath made:
> Thus his name became MAU.'

from THE SPHINX
Oscar Wilde

DAWN follows Dawn and Nights grow old
    and all the while this curious cat
Lies couching on the Chinese mat
    with eyes of satin rimmed with gold

Upon the mat she lies and leers
    and on the tawny throat of her
Flutters the soft and silky fur
    or ripples to her pointed ears.

Come forth, my lovely seneschal!
    so somnolent so statuesque!
Come forth, you exquisite grotesque!
    half woman and half animal!

TO AN ABYSSINIAN CAT
Lynn Hamilton

O STATELY Dreamer, wrapped in meditative mood,
How little you have lost of primal fortitude;
And though from days of Ptolemy you have travelled far,
How little changed from Egypt's goddess Bast you are.

Lost in antiquity the lineage of your sires,
Yet down the ages you have borne their spirit-fires;
Across the desert sand, and over oceans wide,
You came on wingless feet to dwell here at my side.

Best comrade man could have to share the firelight's gleam,
You purr the hours away while lazily I dream.
One with the silent night, your eyes like glowing stars,
Brave warrior, fierce and fleet, you are true son of Mars.

Atop the garden wall, limned 'gainst the mellow moon,
Beneath the same old stars you wail the self-same tune
That your ancestral sire crooned centuries ago
To charm his Desdemona in pagan Cairo.

When goddess Astoreth was wooed by slave and queen,
And *Felis* was a toast along Nile's ageless stream.
Small cat of regal grace, what I would give to share
Your dreams of paradise in olden Egypt where

Your own immortal fame outshone Sahara's sun
A thousand years before Rome's history had begun.
Then on the golden throne of Pharoah you reclined,
Adored by multitudes – within their hearts enshrined.

And you are still adored by doting slaves like me,
Who praise your changeless soul – your passion to be free;
Who feed you purest cream and comb your gleaming fur,
Enchanted by the rhythm of your melodic purr.

Had man your psychic power to look into the past,
Perhaps he would again enthrone the goddess Bast,
And you would rise to claim your heritage of yore –
Your glory that is lost in ancient realms of lore.

from THE DIMINUTIVE LYON
or *CATUS*, THE CAT
William Salmon

II   IT IS bred and is an Inhabitant of almost all Countries in the
World, all *Cats* were at first wild, but were at length tamed by
the industry of Mankind; it is a Beast of prey, even the tame one,
more especially the wild, it being in the opinion of many nothing
but a diminutive Lyon.

IV   It has a broad Face almost like a Lyon, short Ears, large
Whiskers, shining Eyes, short smooth Hair, long Tail, rough
Tongue, and armed on its Feet with Claws, being a crafty, subtle
watchful Creature, very loving and familiar with Man-kind, the
mortal enemy to the Rat, Mouse, and all sorts of Birds, which
it seizes on as its prey. As to its Eyes, Authors say that they shine
in the Night, and see better at the full, and more dimly at the
change of the Moon; as also that the Cat doth vary his Eyes with
the Sun, the Apple of its Eye being long at Sun rise, round
towards Noon, and not to be seen at all at night, but the whole
Eye shining in the night. These appearances of the Cats Eyes I
am sure are true, but whether they answer to the times of the
day, I never observed.

V   It is a neat and cleanly creature, often licking it self, to keep
it fair and clean, and washing its Face with its fore-feet; the best
are such as are of a fair and large kind, and of an exquisite
Tabby color, called *Cyprus* Cats. They usually generate in the
winter Season, making a great noise, go 56 Days or 8 weeks with
young, and bring forth 2, 3, 4, 5, 6, or more at a time, they cover
their excrements, and love to keep their old habitations.

MIAO
Dilys Laing

I PUT down my book
The Meaning of Zen
and see the cat smiling
   into her fur
as she deliberately combs it
   with her pink tongue.

'Cat, I would lend you this
   book to study
but it appears that you have
   already read it.'

She looks up and gives me
   her full gaze.
'Don't be ridiculous,' she purrs.
   'I wrote it.'

LE CHAT NOIR
G.R.Tomson

HALF loving-kindness and half disdain,
Thou comest to my call serenely suave,
With humming speech and gracious gesture grave,

In salutation courtly and urbane.
Yet must I humble me thy grace to gain,
For wiles may win thee, but no arts enslave,
And nowhere gladly thou abidest, save
Where naught disturbs the concord of thy reign,

Sphinx of my quiet hearth who deignst to dwell
Friend of my toil, companion of mine ease,
Thine is the lore of Ra and Rameses;
That men forget dost thou remember well,
Beholden still in blinking reveries,
With sombre sea-green gaze inscrutable.

OUT OF EGYPT
Bayka Russell

A CAT like ebony beneath the trees
Blinks lazily as city daylight dies.
Across impenetrable centuries
I see old Egypt in his widening eyes,
When Pasht, cat-headed goddess of the moon,
Was worshipped near the Nile with ancient rites,
Or by some drowsy, lotus-starred lagoon
Where gathered all her stealthy acolytes.

What called him back, what curious instinct drew
This legendary creature of the dark
To wander like some apparition through
The greening shrubbery of Central Park?
Perhaps this obelisk of age-old fame
Had whispered to him Cleopatra's name.

CATS

A. S. J. Tessimond

CATS, no less liquid than their shadows,
   Offer no angles to the wind.
They slip, diminished, neat, through loopholes
   Less than themselves; will not be pinned

To rules or route for journeys; counter
   Attack with non-resistance; twist
Enticing through the curving fingers
   And leave an angered, empty fist.

They wait, obsequious as darkness,
   Quick to retire, quick to return;
Admit no aim or ethics; flatter
   With reservations; will not learn

To answer to their names; are seldom
   Truly owned till shot and skinned.
Cats, no less liquid than their shadows,
   Offer no angles to the wind.

O LITTLE CAT WITH YELLOW EYES
Helen Vaughn Williams

O LITTLE cat with yellow eyes,
Enthroned upon my garden gate,
Remote, impassive and sedate
And so unutterably wise.

You seem to watch a world that lies
Behind us – where the shadows wait,
O little cat with yellow eyes,
Enthroned upon my garden gate!

Where visions of the past arise,
Of honoured dust and royal state,
And Pharaohs bowed to call you great.

Or are you merely spotting flies,
O little cat with yellow eyes?

THE CAT
Lord Dunsany

I AM not alone in the room:
  A bright intelligence
Watches the fire in the gloom
  Of Winter's imminence;

. . .

Wisdom it has from of yore
  Touching all things that concern it,
And all that I know of its lore
  Is that I shall never learn it.

DECEMBER 1979
Anthony Twentyman

26th THE hard wind roared
And battered
Against the great window
Of my bedroom
Where my cat sang to me
In the darkness
Cats know
What goes on

27th The leaden sky
Pours forth its tears
All the day long
The flooded fields
The broken lanes
The leaking roofs
The wet cat's fur
Bear witness
To what?
Cats know to what

28th Today is different
The moon-white frost upon the ground
As the day lightens
The shaft of sunlight through the broken cloud
The sudden blinding snow
Later the still grey evening
When my cat
Stalks out
Intent upon her secret purpose
Cats know
What's what

CAT AS LIGHT OF THE WORLD
R. K. Meiners

CATS in various times and places
have rearranged the world about them
and gone about saying meow, miaow,
niago, ariri, orare, and even
the seven sacred names of God
to any that would listen.
But my cat moves quietly
through the shelves and papers,
in and out of physic and astronomy,
speaking softly, whewell, whewell,
and occasionally pronouncing, ohm,
as he savours the riches of Liddell and Scott.
Each night he measures light and dark,
tries the sanctuaries of the word,
urging me to contemplate anew
the holy space where all the sciences
and their names are freshly portioned out.

MY ANGORA CAT
W. A. Roberts

NO ONE of all the women I have known
   Has been so beautiful, or proud, or wise
   As this Angora with her amber eyes.
She makes her chosen cushion seem a throne,
   And wears the same voluptuous, slow smile
   She wore when she was worshipped on the Nile.

THE POPE'S CAT
François René de Chateaubriand

MY COMPANION is a large grey and red cat, banded with black. He was born in the Vatican, in the loggia of Raphael. Leo the Twelfth reared him on a fold of his white robe, where I used to look at him with envy when, as ambassador, I received my audiences. The successor of Saint Peter being dead, I inherited the bereaved animal. He is called Micetto, and surnamed 'the Pope's cat', enjoying in that regard much consideration from pious souls. I endeavour to soften his exile, and help him to forget the Sistine Chapel, and the vast dome of Saint Angelo, where, far from earth, he was wont to take his daily promenade.

Grimalkin

INTRODUCTION

And behold
A rakehall cat –
how furtive and acold!

W. E. HENLEY

THERE were bad times for cats under the Tudors and King James I when they suffered obscene persecutions together with the witches they were supposed to serve. Out of terror under torture the old women examinates would confess to any crimes of which they were accused and admit to having rewarded their familiars with their own blood and milk.

Some of this superstitious revulsion lingers in human allergies to cats' fur or in hysterical objection to the sounds they make. The thirteenth-century encyclopaedist, Bartholomew Anglicus, described it: 'He makyth a rufull noise and a gastefulle when he proffereth to fight with another', and marital relations on the tiles at midnight are celebrated by what John Wilson called 'the dismal song of hymeneal bliss' in his *Noctes Ambrosianae.*

In the ancient world the cat was appreciated for his usefulness medicinally. Claudius Galen, a Greek physician of the second century, advised midwives that 'to mix the gall of a cat with the black dung of the same cat burnt under a woman travelling [in travail] with a dead child will cause it presently to come forth', and Agathos recommended a way to ensure pleasant dreams by 'taking a cat black all over and writing on a tablet with a solution of myrrh when pleasant dreams will be put into its mouth'.

The independence of the cat, the wilfulness of his comings in and his goings out, is a reproach to dull humans who cannot but resent it. 'Avaunt Grimalkin' is a natural reaction to what is mysterious and magical beyond their understanding.

THE FAMILIAR
R. W. D. Fuller

WHEN Tabby crouches by the fire,
   Primly a-gaze, her eyes are rings
Of agate flame: and strange desire
   Burns there, and old unholy things.

Surges on dream the lost Delight:
   And off she goes, careering down
The windy archways of the night,
   Afar on flying broomsticks blown.

EXTRACTS FROM TUDOR WITCH TRIALS

Windsor, 1579
... MOTHER Deuell, dwellying nigh the Ponde in Windesore, hath a spirite in the shape of a Blacke Catte, and calleth it Gille, whereby she is aided in her Witchcrafte, and she daiely feedeth it with Milke, mingled with her owne bloud ...

Chelmsford, 1556
[Mother Waterhouse] to trye him what he coulde do wylde him to kyll a hog of her owne, which he dyd, and she gave him for his labour a chicken, which he fryste required of her and a drop of her blod. And thys she gaue him at all times when he dyd anythynge for her, by pricking her hand or face and puttinge the bloud to hys mouth whyche he sucked, and forthwith wold lye downe in his pot againe, wherein she kepte him.

Pitcairn, 1590
[Examinate Agnes Sampson] confessed that she took a cat and christened it, and afterwards bounde to each part of that cat the chiefest parte of a dead man and several joyntes of his bodie. And in the night following, the saide catt was conveyed into the middest of the sea by all the witches, sayling in their riddles or cives [sieves], as is aforesaid, and so left the said cat right before the towne of Leith in Scotland. This doone, there did arise such a tempest in the sea, as a greator hath not bene seene.

THE CAT THAT WALKED BY HIMSELF
Rudyard Kipling

... THE Cat keeps his side of the bargain too.... He will kill mice, and he will be kind to Babies when he is in the house, just as long as they do not pull his tail too hard. But when he has done that, and between times, and when the moon gets up and night comes, he is the Cat that walks by himself, and all places are alike to him. Then he goes out to the Wet Wild Woods or up the Wet Wild Trees or on the Wet Wild Roofs, waving his wild tail and walking by his wild lone.

from TOBERMORY
'Saki'

... OF COURSE I have experimented with thousands of animals, but latterly only with cats, those wonderful creatures which have assimilated themselves so marvellously with our civilization while retaining all their highly developed feral instincts. Here and there among cats one comes across an outstanding superior intellect, just as one does among the ruck of human beings, and when I made the acquaintance of Tobermory a week ago I saw at once that I was in contact with a 'Beyond-cat' of extraordinary intelligence.

THE HOUND PUSS
Stevie Smith

I HAVE a cat: I call him Pumpkin,
A great fat furry purry lumpkin.
Hi-dee-diddle hi-diddle dumpkin.

He sleeps within my bed at night,
His eyes are Mephistopheles-bright:
I dare not look upon their blight.

He stalks me like my angry God,
His gaze is like a fiery rod:
He dines exclusively on cod.

Avaunt, you creeping saviour-devil,
Away with thy angelic evil!

TO A CAT
R. C. K. Ensor

VOLUPTUOUSLY cruel eyes,
I peep into you as a child
Peeps at forbidden mysteries,
Half conscience-bitten, half beguiled.

Your liquid lustre makes for me
A mirror like a witch's bowl:
I see look back unfalteringly
The Demon – who is my soul.

TO A YOUNG CAT IN THE ORCHARD
Frances Cornford

ELEGANT creature with black shoulders bent,
Stalking the bird in song,
To what intent?
Tell what a wild source brims those empty eyes,
What well of shameless light,
Beyond the bounds of Hell or Paradise
Or wrong
Or right.

STRANGE GAMUT
John Wilson

FROM the soft music of the spinning purr,
When no stiff hair disturbs the glossy fur,
The whining wail, so piteous and so faint,
When through the house Puss moves with long complaint.

To that unearthly throttling caterwaul,
When feline legions storm the midnight wall,
And chant, with short snuff and alternate hiss,
The dismal song of hymeneal bliss.

CAT'S PRIDE
Geoffrey Chaucer

For whoso wolde senge a cattes skyn,
Thanne wolde the cate wel dwellen in his in;
And if the cattes skyn by slyk and gay,
She wol not dwelle in house half a day,
But forth she wole, er any day be dawed,
To shewe hir skyn, and goon a-caterwawed.

from DOMBEY AND SON
Charles Dickens

[MRS Pipchin's cat] generally lay coiled up upon the centre foot of the fender purring egotistically and winking at the fire until the contracted pupils of his eyes were like two notes of admiration. The good old lady might have been - not to record it disrespectfully - a witch and Paul and the cat her two familiars, as they all sat by the fire together. It would have been quite in keeping with the appearance of the party if they had all sprung up the chimney in a high wind one night and never been heard of any more....

THE FORMIDABLE 'GYPSY'
Booth Tarkington

His extraordinary size, his daring, and his utter lack of sympathy soon made him the leader – and, at the same time, the terror – of all the loose-lived cats in a wide neighbourhood. He contracted no friendships and had no confidents. He seldom slept in the same place twice in succession, and though he was wanted by the police, he was not found. In appearance he did not lack distinction of an ominous sort; the slow, rhythmic, perfectly controlled mechanism of his tail, as he impressively walked abroad, was incomparably sinister.

THE TOM CAT
Don Marquis

AT MIDNIGHT in the alley
  A Tom-cat comes to wail,
And he chants the hate of a million years
  As he swings his snaky tail.

Malevolent, bony, brindled,
  Tiger and devil and bard,
His eyes are coals from middle of Hell
  And his heart is black and hard.

He twists and crouches and capers
  And bares his curved sharp claws,
And he sings to the stars of the jungle nights
  Ere cities were, or laws.

Beast from a world primeval,
  He and his leaping clan,
When the blotched red moon leers over the roofs
  Give voice to their scorn of man.

He will lie on a rug to-morrow
  And lick his silky fur,
And veil the brute in his yellow eyes
  And play he's tame and purr.

But at midnight in the alley
  He will crouch again and wail,
And beat the time for his demon's song
  With the swing of his demon's tail.

ON THE DEATH OF A CAT
Christina Rossetti

Who shall tell the lady's grief
When her Cat was past relief?
Who shall number the hot tears
Shed o'er her, belov'd for years?
Who shall say the dark dismay
Which her dying caused that day?

. . .

Of a noble race she came,
And Grimalkin was her name.
Young and old full many a mouse
Felt the prowess of her house;
Weak and strong full many a rat
Cowered beneath her crushing pat;
And the birds around the place
Shrank from her too close embrace.
But one night, reft of her strength,
She lay down and died at length:
Lay a kitten by her side
In whose life the mother died.
Spare her line and lineage,
Guard her kitten's tender age,
And that kitten's name as wide
Shall be known as hers that died.
And whoever passes by
The poor grave where Puss doth lie,
Softly, softly let him tread,
Nor disturb her narrow bed.

Gib-Hunter

INTRODUCTION

He was a mighty hunter in his youth
At Polmear all day on the mound, on the pounce
For anything moving, rabbit, or bird, or mouse –

A.L.ROWSE

TOWARDS the cat as hunter the attitude of humans is discriminatory: sorry for the birds but not the worms they kill, sorry for the mice but not the rats. The choice is not rational but sentimental, sometimes aesthetic like having fur, or from sheer hypocrisy.

O wise Azubah, heed not the foolish condemnation of the
mob of men.

The mob who murder the lamb for meat and the seal for vanity.
There have been times when the cat as hunter was valued in economic terms. King Hoel of Wales in the tenth century laid down controlled rates for his services and Sir Richard Whittington's fortune was founded by venturing his cat on a vessel trading to Arabia where it was bought for a great price by a Sheik to hunt down mice in his harem. Even today an allowance is made to sub-post offices towards the keep of a cat and the British Museum's funds provide £50 per annum for each of the six on their establishment pay-roll.
And the attitude of the cat towards all this?

I do not know if mouse or song-bird feels.
I only know they make me light and salutary meals.

from LAWS AND INSTITUTES (*circa* 920 AD)
Hoel Dda (Howell the Good, King of Wales)

The Vendolian Code

The worth of a cat and her teithi [qualities] is this –

1st   The worth of a kitten from the night it is kittened until it shall open its eyes, is a legal penny.

2nd   And from the time that it shall kill mice, twopence.

3rd   And after it shall kill mice, four legal pence: and so it always remains.

4th   Her teithi are to see, to hear, to kill mice, and to have her claws entire...

The Dimetian Code

1st   The worth of a cat that is killed or stolen. Its head is to be put downward upon a clean even floor, with its tail lifted upwards, and thus suspended, whilst wheat is poured about it until the tip of its tail be covered, and that is to be its worth.

2nd   The worth of a common cat is four legal pence.

...

4th   Whosoever shall sell a cat is to answer for her not going a caterwauling every moon ... and that she devour not her kittens and that she have ears, eyes, teeth and nails, and be a good mouser.

DICK WHITTINGTON'S CAT
1641 ballad

. . .

BUT as he went along
   In a fair summer's morne
London bells sweetly rung,
   'Whittington, back return!'

Evermore a sounding so
   'Turn againe Whittington:
For thou in time shall grow
   Lord Mayor of London.'
Whereupon back againe
   Whittington came with speed,
Aprentise to remaine
   As the Lord had decreed.

'Still blessed be the bells'
   (This was his daily song),
'They my good fortune tells
   Most sweetly have they rung.
If God so favour me
   I will not proove unkind;
London my love shall see,
   And my great bounties find.'

But for this happy chance
   Whittington had a cat
Which he a venture sent
   And got his wealth by that
Far from Foreign Land
   Where Rats and Mice abound
They bought him for his cat
   Many a fair thousand pound.

When as they home were come
   With their ships laden so
Whittington's wealth began
   By this cat and thus to grow;
Scullion's life he forsook
   To be a merchant good . . . .

PANGUR BÁN
(Irish ninth-century)

translation by Robin Flower

I AND Pangur Bán, my cat,
'Tis a like task we are at;
Hunting mice is his delight,
Hunting words I sit all night.

Better far than praise of men
'Tis to sit with book and pen;
Pangur bears me no ill will,
He too plies his simple skill.

'Tis a merry thing to see
At our tasks how glad are we,
When at home we sit and find
Entertainment to our mind.

Oftentimes a mouse will stray
In the hero Pangur's way;
Oftentimes my keen thought set
Takes a meaning in its net.

'Gainst the wall he sets his eye
Full and fierce and sharp and sly;
'Gainst the wall of knowledge I
All my little wisdom try.

When a mouse darts from its den,
O how glad is Pangur then!
O what gladness do I prove
When I solve the doubts I love!

So in peace our tasks we ply,
Pangur Bán, my cat and I;
In our hearts we find our bliss,
I have mine and he has his.

Practice every day has made
Pangur perfect in his trade;
I get wisdom day and night
Turning darkness into light.

MY CAT
Philip Sidney

I HAVE (and long shall have) a white, great nimble cat,
A King upon a mouse, a strong foe to the rat.
Fine eares, long taile he hath, with Lions curbèd clawe,
Which oft he lifteth up and stayes his lifted pawe.
Deep musing to himselfe, which after mewing showes,
Till with lickt bearde his eye of fire espie his foes.

AZUBAH
Michael Joseph

THEY call you cruel, Azubah; they who prepare the patient
ox for slaughter, who hunt the timid stag for sport.
I do not understand. Is water cruel that flows?
Is the wind cruel that destroys the tender blossoms?

They say you torture wantonly, they who teach the dog
to rend the panting fox. They do not understand you must,
or lose your heritage of freedom. The practice
of your deadly art must be maintained or you in turn
will perish with your race. This they do not understand.

Our human laws! What mockery are they, whence men destroy
their fellows with bullet, bomb and poison gas.
Humanity has yet to learn protection from itself.

O wise Azubah, heed not the foolish condemnation of the mob
of men. Regard their judgment with an indifferent eye;
pursue your prey at will. If it will be cruelty
to preserve your kind, be generously cruel.

All I ask is your return to me when the chase tires you.
Come then, and rest, for no reproach from me shall
greet your coming. Here is one who understands.

THE TRAITOR CAT
Thomas Wyatt

UNDER a stool she spied two steaming eyes
In a round head, with sharp ears. In France
Was never mouse so feared, for the unwise
Had not seen such a beast before.
Yet had nature taught her after her guise
To know her foe, and dread him evermore.
The town mouse fled, she knew whither to go;
Th'other had no shift, but wonders sore;
Feared of her life, at home she wished her tho,
And to the door, alas, as she did skip,
Th'heaven it would, lo, and eke her chance was so
At the threshold her sely foot did trip;
And ere she might recover it again,
The traitor cat had caught her by the hip,
And made her there against her will remain.

ON A CAT AGEING
Alexander Gray

HE BLINKS upon the hearth-rug
And yawns in deep content,
Accepting all the comforts
That Providence has sent.

Louder he purrs, and louder,
In one glad hymn of praise,
For all the night's adventures,
For quiet, restful days.

Life will go on for ever,
With all that cat can wish;
Warmth, and the glad procession
Of fish, and milk and fish.

Only – the thought disturbs him –
He's noticed once or twice,
That times are somehow breeding
A nimbler race of mice.

THE CAT AND THE MICE
Aesop

A CAT, grown feeble with age, and no longer able to hunt for mice as she was wont to do, sat in the sun and bethought herself how she might entice them within reach of her paws.

The idea came to her that if she would suspend herself by the hind legs from a peg in the closet wall, the mice, believing her to be dead, no longer would be afraid of her. So, at great pains and with the assistance of a torn pillow case she was able to carry out her plan.

But before the mice could approach within range of the innocent-looking paws a wise old gaffer-mouse whispered to his friends: 'Keep your distance, my friends. Many a bag have I seen in my day, but never one with a cat's head at the bottom of it.'

Then turning to the uncomfortable feline, he said: 'Hang there, good madam, as long as you please, but I would not trust myself within reach of you though you were stuffed with straw.'

Application HE WHO IS ONCE DECEIVED IS DOUBLY CAUTIOUS

MIN MISSES A MOUSE
Henry David Thoreau

MIN caught a mouse, and was playing with it in the yard. It had got away from her once or twice and she had caught it again, and now it was stealing off again, as she was complacently watching it with her paws tucked under her, when her friend, Riorden, a stout cock, stepped up inquisitively, looked down at the mouse with one eye, turning its head, then picked it up by the tail, gave it two or three whacks on the ground, and giving it a dexterous toss in the air, caught the mouse in its open mouth. It went, head foremost and alive, down Riorden's capacious throat in the twinkling of an eye, never again to be seen in this world; Min all the while, with paws comfortably tucked under her, looking on unconcerned. What did one mouse matter, more or less, to her? The cock walked off amid the currant-bushes, stretched his neck up and gulped once or twice, and the deed was accomplished. Then he crowed lustily in celebration of the exploit. It might be set down among the *Gesta gallorum*. There were several human witnesses. It is a question whether Min ever understood where that mouse went to. She sits composedly sentinel, with paws tucked under her, a good part of her days at present, by some ridiculous little hole, the possible entry of a mouse.

RONDEAU FOR A CAT
R. W. Ketton-Cremer

THERE is a Cat, his master's chief delight –
A Cat of strength and beauty, speed and might,
  In whose great eyes a depth of green flame glows;
  His silken fur is black as night, and snows
Cover his throat and feet with purest white.

And when he crouches on a branch's height,
Watching the swallows in their wheeling flight,
  Each bird knows well that where that black form shows,
                              There is a Cat.

And in the evening through the stealthy light,
He stalks on silent feet, eyes gleaming bright;
  And all the world, awake and wary, knows –
  Each bird, mouse, rabbit – that a Peril goes
About the land: dark brother to the Night,
                              There is a Cat!

FIVE EYES

Walter de la Mare

In HANS' old mill his three black cats
Watch the bins for the thieving rats.
Whisker and claw, they crouch in the night,
Their five eyes smouldering green and bright:
Squeaks from the flour sacks, squeaks from where
The cold wind stirs on the empty stair,
Squeaking and scampering everywhere.
Then down they pounce, now in, now out,
At whisking tail, and sniffing snout;
While lean old Hans he snores away
Till peep of light at break of day;
Then up he climbs to his creaking mill,
Out come his cats all grey with meal –
Jekkel, and Jessup, and one-eyed Jill.

THE MANCIPLE'S TALE
Geoffrey Chaucer

LAT take a cat and fostre hym wel with milk
And tendré flessch and make his couche of silk,
And lat hym seen a mous go by the wal,
Anon he weyvith milk and flessch and al,
And every deyntee that is in that hous,
Swich appetit hath he to ete a mous.

ON PUBLIC POLICY
Adlai Stevenson

I CANNOT agree that it should be the declared public policy of Illinois that a cat visiting a neighbour's yard or crossing the highway is a public nuisance. It is the nature of cats to do a certain amount of unescorted roaming. Many live with their owners in apartments or other restricted premises, and I doubt if we want to make their every brief foray an opportunity for a small-game hunt by zealous citizens with traps or otherwise.

I am afraid this bill could only create discord, recrimination and enmity.

Also consider the owner's dilemma: To escort a cat abroad on a leash is against the nature of a cat, and to permit it to venture forth for exercise unattended into a night of new dangers is against the nature of the owner.

Moreover, cats perform useful service, particularly in rural areas, in combating rodents – work they necessarily perform alone and without regard for property lines.

We are all interested in protecting certain varieties of birds. That cats destroy some birds, I well know, but I believe this legislation would further but little the worthy cause to which its proponents give such unselfish effort. The problem of a cat versus bird is as old as time. If we attempt to resolve it by legislation, who knows but what we may be called upon to take sides as well in the age-old problem of dog versus cat, bird versus bird or even bird versus worm.

Tabby

INTRODUCTION

The cat's rolled round in vacant chair
or leaping childrens' knees to lair,
or purring on the warmer hearth
sweet chorus to the cricket's mirth.

JOHN CLARE

TABBY, the homely Moggy, is the ordinary cat, if any cat were ordinary. He may be of no registered breed but he is the ancestor of them all.

More than most he expects sustenance and solicitude. When he chooses to join the family at tea-time, he looks for the saucer that

like a full moon
Descends at last from the clouds above.

(But surely it must be 'at once' and not 'at last' in any well cat-regulated household?) He then retires to sleep it off – whatever he has been doing.

Tabby can return affection with compassion. The Earl of Southampton imprisoned in the Tower was cheered by his cat which contrived to find a way down into his cell – or was it that he scented good hunting-ground? He is as different from Puss as are his families. In Dame Ivy Compton-Burnett's *Mother and Son* the two households are revealed in the names they give their cats. There is the beloved Plautus, so called because he has not written plays that are any good either, and, across a social and intellectual divide, there is Tabbikins, relegated to the back. The difference is in the diminutive.

TO A CAT
A.C.*Swinburne*

STATELY, kindly, lordly friend
    Condescend
Here to sit by me, and turn
Glorious eyes that smile and burn,
Golden eyes, love's lustrous meed,
On the golden page I read.

All your wondrous wealth of hair,
    Dark and fair,
Silken-shaggy, soft and bright
As the clouds and beams of night,
Pays my reverent hand's caress
Back with friendlier gentleness.

Dogs may fawn on all and some
    As they come;
You, a friend of loftier mind,
Answer friends alone in kind.
Just your foot upon my hand
Softly bids it understand.

JEREMIAH, THE TABBY CAT
A.L.Rowse

WHILE you clamber over the blue gate in the garden,
In the sunlit garden I
Already arrived am before you: while
In a flash of the eye
You are suspended in your leap, an invert body
With light panther movement,
Against the blue ground of the gate. And then,
Unconscious cinema-actor, you cross your stage,
The little plot where light cuts the shade like a jewel,
Of what intent?
Your eyes are amber in the sun, flashing
From the cushioned tuft of harebells
And calceolarias.
Now you thread the intricate pattern
Of long garden stems and stems of shadows,
And cross the lawn:
Your subtle flanks serpentine, you tread
Stealthy and secret, of who knows
What generations of great jungle cats?
And so you reach the undergrowth of the sycamore;
Nor pause to hear me calling from the window
Whence sight of you I lose,
Your dappled side lost in the camouflage of dappled shadow:
And you have left the sunlit garden
For who knows what obscure instinctive memories of lost
generations of great cats?

A STROLL WITH EZRA POUND
William Butler Yeats

SOMETIMES about ten o'clock at night I accompany him to a street where there are hotels upon one side, upon the other palm-trees and the sea, and there, taking out of his pocket bones and pieces of meat, he begins to call the cats. He knows all their histories – the brindled cat looked like a skeleton until he began to feed it; that fat grey is an hotel proprietor's favourite, it never begs from the guests' tables and it turns cats that do not belong to the hotel out of the garden; this black cat and that grey cat over there fought on the roof of a four-storied house some weeks ago, fell off, a whirling ball of claws and fur, and now avoid each other. Yet now that I recall the scene I think that he has no affection for cats – 'some of them so ungrateful', a friend says – he never nurses the café cat, I cannot imagine him with a cat of his own. Cats are oppressed, dogs terrify them, landladies starve them, boys stone them, everybody speaks of them with contempt. If they were human beings we could talk of their oppressors with a studied violence, add our strength to theirs, even organise the oppressed and like good politicians sell our charity for power . . .

ON THE DEATH OF A FAVOURITE CAT, DROWNED IN A TUB OF GOLD FISHES
Thomas Gray

'TWAS on a lofty vase's side,
Where China's gayest art had dy'd
  The azure flowers that blow;
Demurest of the tabby kind,
The pensive Selima, reclined,
  Gaz'd on the lake below.

Her conscious tail her joy declar'd;
The fair round face, the snowy beard,
  The velvet of her paws,
Her coat, that with the tortoise vies,
The ears of jet, and emerald eyes.
  She saw; and purr'd applause.

. . .

The hapless Nymph with wonder saw:
A whisker first, and then a claw,
  With many an ardent wish,
She stretch'd in vain to reach the prize.
What female heart can gold despise?
  What Cat's averse to fish?

Presumptuous Maid! With looks intent,
Again she stretch'd, again she bent,
  Nor knew the gulf between.
(Malignant Fate sat by and smil'd.)
The slipp'ry verge her feet beguil'd,
  She tumbled headlong in.

Eight times emerging from the flood
She mew'd to ev'ry wat'ry God,
  Some speedy aid to send.

No Dolphin came, no Nereid stirr'd:
Nor cruel *Tom*, nor *Susan* heard.
  A Fav'rite has no friend!

  . . .

TO A CAT WHICH DID NOT DROWN
IN A BOWL OF GOLD FISH
Albert Edmund Trombly

NOT one of your nine lives you lost in this adventure,
Not one; although if she had guessed what you were at,
For all her love of you, your mistress might have shorn you
Of one or two of the nine with a cuff and a crackling *scat!*

If not a model cat, at any rate a modern:
In getting what you want you have such fetching ways.
And then you had the sense or luck to choose a smaller
Bowl than chose that elegized cat of Thomas Gray's.

Not witness to the foray – and much do I regret it –
But knowing you so well I can vividly surmise
Just how you sat beside the bowl with quivering whiskers,
Tail twitching, very devil in your eyes.

And how you curled your paw – not so unlike a fishhook
But four times better barbed – cautiously, then a flash!
Aha, you had one, had you? Or did the rogues elude you
Time and again before you could tuck them under your sash?

When mistress happened by a little later – horrors!
No goldfish in the bowl or out; and mistress cried.
While you hidden safely away behind the fringe of the sofa
Were washing your face of the smell of the sin you were
                            trying to hide.

CAT
C. Day-Lewis

TEARAWAY kitten or staid mother of fifty,
Persian, Chinchilla, Siamese
Or backstreet brawler – you all have a tiger in your blood
And eyes opaque as the sacred mysteries.

The hunter's instinct sends you pouncing, dallying,
Formal and wild as a temple dance.
You take from men what is due – the fireside saucer,
And give him his – a purr of tolerance.

Like poets you wrap your solitude around you
And catch your meaning unawares:
With consequential trot or frantic tarantella
You follow up your top-secret affairs.

Simpkin, our pretty cat, assumes my lap
As a princess her rightful throne,
Pads round and drops asleep there. Each is a familiar
Warmth to the other, each no less alone.

MOHAMMET AND HIS CAT
Pierre Loti

How well I can understand Mohammet, who, in response to the
chant of the muezzin summoning him to prayers, cut off with a
pair of scissors the hem of his cloak before rising to his feet for
fear of disturbing his cat, which had settled down thereon to
sleep.

THE CAT BY THE FIRE
Leigh Hunt

BEAUTIFUL present sufficingness of a cat's imagination! Confined to the snug circle of her own sides, and the two next inches of rug or carpet ... Anon, she scratches her neck with a foot of rapid delight, leaning her head towards it, and shutting her eyes half to accommodate the action of the skin and half to enjoy the luxury. She then rewards her paws with a few more touches – look at the action of her head and neck, how pleasing it is, the ears pointed forward, and the neck gently arching to and fro. Finally, she gives a sneeze, and another twist of mouth and whiskers, and then, curling her tail towards her front claws, settles herself on her hind quarters in an attitude of bland meditation.

from A LETTER
The Reverend R.S.Hawker, Vicar of Morwenstow

IN SPRING when he [Granfer] finds a bird's nest, he brings the young ones in his mouth, one at a time and drops them unhurt by my chair. A whole nest of the large-size Tom-tit that he so served and carried back, lived to fly away, Granfer being shut up till they were fledged. He has brought up a young mole and a frog – a most intelligent cat.

from WAR CAT
Dorothy L. Sayers

I AM sorry, my little cat, I am sorry –
if I had it, you should have it;
but there is a war on.

No, there are no table scraps;
there was only an omelette
made from dehydrated eggs,
and baked apples to follow, and we finished it all.
The butcher has no lights,
the fishmonger has no cods' heads –
there is nothing for you
but cat-biscuit
and those remnants of yesterday's ham;
you must do your best with it.

. . .

Mistress I do my best for the war-effort;
I killed four mice last week,
and yesterday I caught a young stoat.
You stroked and praised me,
you called me a clever cat.
What have I done to offend you?
I am industrious, I earn my keep.
I am not like the parrot, who sits there
using bad language and devouring
parrot-seed at eight-and-sixpence a pound
without working for it.

. . .

Cat with the innocent face
What can I say?
Everything is so very hard on everybody.
If you were a little Greek cat,
or a little Polish cat,
there would be nothing for you at all,
not even cat-food:
indeed, you would be lucky
if you were not eaten yourself.

. . .

Wait only a little
and I will go to the butcher
and see if by any chance
he can produce some fragments of the insides of something.

[The cat then jumps on the table and eats up the rejected pieces
put out for the hens.]

Nevertheless,
although you have made a fool of me,
yet, bearing in mind your pretty wheedling ways
(not to mention the four mice and the immature stoat),
and having put on my hat to go to the butcher's,
I may as well go.

from LIFE OF JOHNSON
James Boswell

I NEVER shall never forget the indulgence with which he treated Hodge, his cat; for whom he himself used to go out and buy oysters, lest the servants having that trouble should take a dislike to the poor creature. I am, unluckily, one of those who have an antipathy to a cat, so that I am uneasy when in the room with one; and I own, I frequently suffered a good deal from the presence of this same Hodge. I recollect him one day scrambling up Dr Johnson's breast, apparently with much satisfaction, while my friend, smiling and half-whistling, rubbed down his back, and pulled him by the tail; and when I observed he was a fine cat, saying, 'Why, yes, Sir, but I have had cats whom I liked better than this;' and then, as if perceiving Hodge to be out of countenance, adding, 'but he is a very fine cat, a very fine cat indeed.'

LADY HOLLAND'S CAT
Thomas Creevey

LADY Holland, in addition to all her former insults upon the town, has set up a huge CAT, which is never permitted to be out of her sight and to whose vagaries she demands unqualified submission from all her visitors. Rogers, it seems, has already sustained considerable injury in a personal affair with the animal. Brougham only keeps him, or HER, at arm's length by snuff, and Luttrell has sent in a formal resignation of all further visits till this odious new favourite is dismissed from the Cabinet.

CAT
Michael Hamburger

UNFUSSY lodger, she knows what she wants and gets it:

Food, cushions, fires, the run of the garden.
I, her night porter in the small hours,
Don't bother to grumble, grimly let her in.

To that coldness she purrs assent,
Eats her fill and outwits me,
Plays hide and seek in the dark house.

Only at times, by chance meeting the gaze
Of her amber eyes that rest on me
As on a beech-bole, on bracken or meadow grass
I'm moved to celebrate the years between us,
The farness and the nearness:
My fingers graze her head.
To that fondness she purrs assent.

HINTS FOR CAT-LOVERS
Edith Benedict Hawes

FEED a yellow cat from willow pattern, – blue.
Give a black cat his supper from a yellow bowl.
Let the Maltese have a gaudy dish, – tomato-red will do.
And always feed white kittens from Dresden china.

Something modernistic for the calico cat;
But oh! for a gray Angora, with a white breast,
There is no scheme for soft contentment that
Outdoes a bit of rosy salmon in gray Wedgwood ware!

MRS DILKE'S CATS
John Keats

MRS DILKE has two Cats – a Mother and a Daughter – now the Mother is a tabby and the daughter a black and white like the spotted child – Now it appears quite ominous to me, for the doors of both houses are opened frequently – so that there is a complete thoroughfare for both Cats (there being no board up to the contrary) they may one and several of them come into my room *ad libitum*. But no – the Tabby only comes – whether from sympathy from Ann the Maid or me I can not tell. . . . The Cat is not an old Maid herself – her daughter is a proof of it – I have questioned her – I have look'd at the lines of her paw – I have felt her pulse – to no purpose. Why should the *old* Cat come to me? I ask myself – and myself has not a word to answer.

TO A CAT
John Keats

CAT! who hast passed thy grand climacteric,
How many mice and rats hast in thy days
Destroyed? – How many tit-bits stolen? Gaze
With those bright languid segments green, and prick
Those velvet ears – but pr'ythee do not stick
Thy latent talons in me – and upraise
Thy gentle mew – and tell me all thy frays
Of fish and mice, and rats and tender chick.

Nay, look not down, nor lick thy dainty wrists –
For all the wheezy asthma, – and for all
Thy tail's tip is nick'd off – and though the fists
Of many a maid have given thee a maul,
Still is that fur as soft as when the lists
In youth thou enter'dst on glass bottled wall.

ATOSSA
Matthew Arnold

THOU hast seen Atossa sage
Sit for hours beside thy cage;
Thou wouldst chirp, thou foolish bird,
Flutter, chirp – she never stirr'd!
What were now these toys to her?
Down she sank amid her fur;
Eyed thee with a soul resign'd –
And thou deemedst cats were kind!
– Cruel, but composed and bland,
Dumb, inscrutable and grand,
So Tiberius might have sat,
Had Tiberius been a cat.

from A LETTER, 1868
Matthew Arnold

I HAVE just been called to the door by the sweet voice of Tossa, whose morning proceedings are wonderful – she has just jumped on my lap, and her beautiful tail has made this smudge. I was going to say that she sleeps on an armchair before the drawing-room fire and enters Flu's room with Eliza regularly at halfpast seven. Then she comes to my room and gives a mew: and then, especially if I let her in and go on writing without taking notice of her, there is a real demonstration of affection for five minutes such as never again occurs in the day. She purrs, she walks round and round me. She jumps on my lap, she turns to me and rubs her head and nose against my chin: she opens her mouth and raps her pretty white teeth against my pen: then she jumps down, settles herself before the fire, and never shows any more affection that day.

THE SILVER CAT
Humbert Wolfe

HE DREW the curtains, and at that
from where he lay, a silver cat
rose, stretched his silky paws to yawn
at the geraniums of the dawn,
whose petals splashed the window. Then
curls himself to sleep again.

LAST WORDS TO A DUMB FRIEND
Thomas Hardy

PET was never mourned as you
Purrer of the spotless hue,
Plumy tail, and wistful gaze
While you humoured our queer ways,
Or outshrilled your morning call
Up the stairs and through the hall –
Foot suspended in its fall –
While, expectant, you would stand
Arched, to meet the stroking hand;
Till your way you chose to wend
Yonder, to your tragic end.

. . .

From the chair, whereon he sat
Sweep his fur, nor wince thereat;
Rake his little pathways out
Mid the bushes roundabout;
Smooth away his talons' mark
From the claw-worn pine-tree bark,
Where he climbed as dusk embrowned
Waiting us who loitered round.

. . .

Housemate, I can think you still
Bounding to the window-sill,
Over which I vaguely see
Your small mound beneath the tree,
Showing in the autumn shade
That you moulder where you played.

Puss

INTRODUCTION

To live a simple pussy by her side
Was nobler far than to be deified.

La Mothe le Vayer,
Translated by Edmund Gosse

THE case of pussy is often sad for he, usually called 'she', may be
the beloved pet abandoned when he grows up or the animal
insulted by people who say they like cats when they are kittens
but prefer dogs. He is often a victim to his own charms, celebrated
by Joanna Baillie in the early nineteenth century:

Wanter droll whose harmless play
Beguiles the rustic's closing day.

He is expected to entertain the company:

Come show thy tricks and sportive graces
Thus circled round with merry faces.

A later Victorian, C.S.Calverley, was more realistic:

They tell me I am beautiful; they praise my silken hair,
My little feet that silently slip on from stair to stair

but when he is older it is different – he gets the blame for every
accident:

Should china fall or chandeliers or anything but stocks
Nay, stocks when they're in flower pots – the cat expects
hard knocks.

No wonder he is often addressed as 'Poor Pussy', but the cat-
lover knows beneath the pathetic prettiness he has still the spit
and spirit of Mehitaphel, the female,

brief centuries
ago one of old
king
tut
ankh
amen's favourite
queens.

Back to Bast, the Sphinx.

CAT HOROSCOPE
Ann Currah

GEMINI (MAY 21–JUNE 20)   Essentially the kitten-cat, that changeful pussy with the gift of eternal youth. So far as felines fret, Gemini frets. He desires change of scene, balls of wool; is much in demand for TV Commercials; is incorrigibly bossy. (Best owners: Libra, Aquarius, but never Taurus.)

SCORPIO (OCTOBER 23–NOVEMBER 22)   Hidden beneath his prettily patterned fur lurks enough power for a fleet of bulldozers. Nobody ever got the better of this cat. He sums you up from the start. A hospitable cat, usually at your expense; likely to expect you to maintain his mate. (Best owners: Cancer, Pisces.)

A SIMPLE PUSSY

La Mothe le Vayer, translated by E. Gosse

Puss passer-by, within this simple tomb
Lies one whose life fell Atropos hath shred;
The happiest cat on earth hath heard her doom,
And sleeps for ever in a marble bed.
Alas! what long delicious days I've seen!
O cats of Egypt, my illustrious sires,
You who on altars, bound with garlands green,
Have melted hearts, and kindled fond desires,
Hymns in your praise were paid, and offerings too,
But I'm not jealous of those rights divine.
Since Ludovisa loved me, close and true,
Your ancient glory was less proud than mine.
To live a simple pussy by her side
Was nobler far than to be deified.

ST JEROME AND HIS LION
Anon.

ST JEROME in his study kept a great big cat,
It's always in his pictures, with its feet upon the mat.
Did he give it milk to drink, in a little dish?
When it came to Fridays did he give it fish?
If I lost my little cat, I'd be sad without it:
I should ask St Jeremy what to do about it:
I should ask St Jeremy, just because of that,
For he's the only saint I know who kept a pussy cat.

from THROUGH THE LOOKING-GLASS
Lewis Carroll

THE way Dinah washed her children's faces was this: first she held the poor thing down by its ear with one paw, and then with the other paw she rubbed its face all over, the wrong way, beginning at the nose: and just now, as I said, she was hard at work on the white kitten, which was lying quite still and trying to purr – no doubt feeling that it was all meant for its good.

But the black kitten had been finished with earlier in the afternoon, and so, while Alice was sitting curled up in a corner of the great arm-chair, half talking to herself and half asleep, the kitten had been having a grand game of romps with the ball of worsted Alice had been trying to wind up, and had been rolling it up and down till it had all come undone again; and there it was, spread over the hearth-rug, all knots and tangles, with the kitten running after its own tail in the middle.

'Oh, you wicked wicked little thing!' cried Alice, catching up the kitten, and giving it a little kiss to make it understand that it was in disgrace. 'Really, Dinah ought to have taught you better manners! You *ought*, Dinah, you know you ought!' she added, looking reproachfully at the old cat, and speaking in as cross a voice as she could manage.

from THE OWL AND THE PUSSYCAT
Edward Lear

THE Owl and the Pussycat went to sea
   In a beautiful pea-green boat,
They took some honey, and plenty of money,
   Wrapped up in a five pound note.
The Owl looked up to the stars above,
   And sang to a small guitar,
'O lovely Pussy, O Pussy, my love,
   What a beautiful Pussy you are,
      You are,
      You are!
   What a beautiful Pussy you are!'

from A LETTER TO
MRS PATTERSON, 2 OCTOBER 1908
Mark Twain

THE contents of your letter are very pleasant and very welcome, and I thank you for them, sincerely. If I can find a photograph of my 'Tammany' and her kittens, I will enclose it in this. One of them likes to be crammed into a corner-pocket of the billiard table – which he fits as snugly as does a finger in a glove and then he watches the game (and obstructs it) by the hour, and spoils many a shot by putting out his paw and changing the direction of a passing ball. Whenever a ball is in his arms, or so close to him that it cannot be played upon without risk of hurting him, the player is privileged to remove it to any one of the 3 spots that chances to be vacant....

from A LETTER TO
BERNARD BARTON, 11 APRIL 1844
Edward Fitzgerald

... THANK Miss Barton much for the *kit*: if it is but a *kit*: my old woman [housekeeper] is a great lover of cats, and hers has just *kitted*, and a wretched little blind puling tabby lizard of a thing was to be saved from the pail for me: but if Miss Barton's is a *kit*, I will gladly have it: and my old lady's shall be disposed of – not to the pail. . . .

TO FLIP
Anthea Lahr, aged five

O IDIOTIC cat
Who sits on a mat
On a dark winter's night.
You really are so sweet
And it's so much of a treat
To have a little cat like you.
You like little mice
You think them very nice
But you think moles better still.
When you were a kitten
I wore a little mitten
To stop you scratching me.

ADVENTURES IN LONDON
Nursery Rhyme

PUSSY Cat, Pussy Cat, where have you been?
I've been up to London to visit the Queen!

Pussy Cat, Pussy Cat, what did you there?
I frightened a little mouse under her chair.

PART SONG
Anon.

I WISH she wouldn't ask me if
I love the kitten more than her.
Of course I love her –
          But I love the kitten too,
And it has fur...

MY CAT AND I
Alan Mathews

WHEN the clock uncovers me
and the day lies mean and flat,
I wrap myself in solitude
and breakfast with my cat.

High on kitchen stools we perch,
metabolism thin,
and ponder on the fates that move
the world of mice and men.

He understands me well, my cat.
He makes no smart replies.
Instinctive wisdom lies behind
his tranquil slitted eyes.

The monstrous tensions of our race
somehow he comprehends,
and how life's great simplicities
evade his giant friends.

So with his furred contentment
he absorbs my edge of pain,
assuring with a rounded purr
that good will rise again.

Restored, I pat him '*au revoir*';
he bumps me with his head.
I hustle out to earn a bob.
He strolls to find a bed.

A CAT-LOVER'S NIGHTMARE
Margaret Rawlings

CRYING, as if left out in ice and snow,
Neglected, bound, and left to die – my cat,
My fed cat, hypocrite, invades my bed
And claws and purrs and kneads and growls for food
At dawn – a winter's dawn at that! Oh cat
Oh welcome blessed evil fiend and friend –
  I really thought you were left out to die
  Neglected, starved. If you had not returned
  How would I ever know how you had died?

FELIX
Shirley Williams
(from a BBC TV interview)

WELL, there were little bits of eccentricity ... My father had
an alcoholic cat - this was an extremely handsome black cat
with very bright green eyes and he used to wake my father up
every morning, mostly by sitting on his face which I wouldn't
have liked very much but it always woke my father up, and the
cat was very attached to my father and used to follow my father
around wherever my father went, like a dog does, you know, he
would go to heel. But unfortunately the drink got him because
at the bottom of our road there is a pub and the people in the
pub would always give this cat who was called Felix very large
plates of beer and Felix was extremely disposed to Newcastle
Brown and other strong beers. After about two years he simply
lapsed and went to live at the pub permanently - he always
greeted my father when my father came in to have a drink which
he mostly did after Church on Sunday, but the cat would not
leave and would not return home. I am afraid he was a complete
delinquent - he was lost.

EPITAPH
Anthony Twentyman

GREAT Pussy lies beneath the sod
Our lamentations rise
But Pussy now is near to God
So let us dry our eyes
For think how happy He must be
With Pussy in His arms
For surely He, no more than we,
Could e'er resist his charms

Tailpiece

CAT JEOFFRY
Christopher Smart

FOR I will consider my Cat Jeoffry.

For he is the servant of the Living God, duly and daily serving
him.

For at the first glance of the glory of God in the East he
worships in his way.

For this is done by wreathing his body seven times round with
elegant quickness.

For then he leaps up to catch the musk, which is the blessing
of God upon his prayer.

For he rolls upon the prank to work it in.

For having done duty and received blessing he begins to
consider himself.

For this he performs in ten degrees.

For first he looks upon his fore-paws to see if they are clean.

For secondly he kicks up behind to clear away there.

For thirdly he works it upon stretch with the fore-paws
extended.

For fourthly he sharpens his paws with wood.

For fifthly he washes himself.

For sixthly he rolls upon wash.

For seventhly he fleas himself, that he may not be interrupted
upon the beat.

For eighthly he rubs himself against a post.

For ninthly he looks up for his instructions.

For tenthly he goes in quest of food.

For having consider'd God and himself he will consider his
neighbour.

. . .

For the Cherub Cat is a term of the Angel Tiger.

For he has the subtlety and hissing of a serpent, which in
goodness he suppresses.

For he will not do destruction, if he is well-fed, neither will he
spit without provocation.

For he purrs in thankfulness, when God tells him he's a good
Cat.

For he is an instrument for the children to learn benevolence
upon.

For every house is incompleat without him and a blessing is
lacking in the spirit.

. . .

For God has blessed him in the variety of his movements.

For, tho' he cannot fly, he is an excellent clamberer.

For his motions upon the face of the earth are more than any
other quadruped.

ACKNOWLEDGMENTS

I AM very grateful to friends who have contributed their poems to this anthology: Dr Leslie Rowse, Miss Margaret Rawlings, Mr Anthony Twentyman, ARBS and to the Rt. Hon. Mrs Shirley Williams for an extract from her broadcast interview. I must also express my appreciation to the Hon. Senator Adlai E. Stevenson for the quotation from a speech by his father when Governor of Illinois; also to Professor Christopher Cornford, Lord Dunsany, and the late Hon. Mrs Anthea Hastings for permissions kindly granted; to Dr Park Honan for several helpful suggestions, and to Mrs Falkus for considerable patience in editing.

I was given a copy of *Sophisti-Cats* by the late Martin Secker and should like to pay tribute here to his unfailing kindness and encouragement to me as to many others. I regret that I was unable to trace the authors of some poems reproduced from it and hope they will accept my apologies. This also applies to others I may have inadvertently omitted to acknowledge.

Thanks are due to the following for permission to reproduce work for which they hold the copyright:

Autolycus Press and Hubert Nicholson for 'Cats' by A.S.J. Tessimond

Beloit Poetry Journal, Wisconsin, U.S.A. for 'Cat as Light of the World' by R.K. Meiners

British Broadcasting Corporation for extract by Rt. Hon. Shirley Williams, P.C. from Michael Parkinson Show, BBC TV, 22 February 1980

Cornford, Christopher, for 'Cat in the Orchard' by Frances Cornford and Bircham and Co., Trustees for Cornford Estates

Dresser, Chapman & Grimes, Publishers, Woburn, Mass., U.S.A. for information about the firm of Chapman & Grimes, Inc. purchased by them in 1958, but unable to supply names of *Sophisti-Cats* authors

Faber and Faber Limited, for lines from T.S. Eliot's *Old Possum's Book of Practical Cats*

Geidt, Lucy, of the BBC for transcribing the Shirley Williams interview

Gray, John, for 'On a Cat Ageing' by Sir Alexander Gray

Harrap, George G. and Co. Ltd for Dorothy L. Sayers' poem 'War Cat'

Macgibbon, James (Executor for the late Stevie Smith)

Mathews, Alan, for 'My Cat and I' from 'Something to Read when there's Nothing to Drink'

Meiners, R.K. see Beloit Poetry Journal, Wisconsin, U.S.A.

Nicholson, Hubert and Autolycus Press for 'Cats' by A.S.J. Tessimond

Peters, A.D. and Co. Ltd, for 'Cat' by C. Day-Lewis and 'A Stroll with Ezra Pound' by W.B. Yeats

Royal Literary Fund for 'Rondeau for a Cat' by R.W. Ketton-Cremer

Rushton, Christopher, for photograph of cat with the author

Smith, Stevie, from *Collected Poems* (Allen Lane) see MacGibbon, James

Society of Authors as representatives of the Literary Trustees of Walter de la Mare

Sophisti-Cats, edited by Lynn Hamilton. See Dresser, Chapman & Grimes

Watt, A.P., for 'The Cat that Walked by Himself' from *Just So Stories* by Rudyard Kipling

Wolfe, Ann, for 'A Silver Cat' by Humbert Wolfe

Yeats, M.B. for permission to use W.B. Yeats passage

INDEX OF AUTHORS